Native Americans

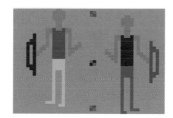

Huron

Barbara A. Gray-Kanatiiosh

ABDO Publishing Company

visit us at
www.abdopub.com

Published by ABDO Publishing Company, 4940 Viking Drive, Suite 622, Edina, Minnesota 55435. Copyright © 2004 by Abdo Consulting Group, Inc. International copyrights reserved in all countries. No part of this book may be reproduced in any form without written permission from the publisher.

Printed in the United States.

Cover Photo: Corbis
Interior Photos: Corbis pp. 4, 28, 29, 30
Illustrations: David Kanietakeron Fadden pp. 7, 9, 11, 13, 15, 17, 19, 21, 23, 25, 27
Editors: Kate A. Conley, Jennifer R. Krueger, Kristin Van Cleaf
Art Direction & Maps: Neil Klinepier

Library of Congress Cataloging-in-Publication Data

Gray-Kanatiiosh, Barbara A., 1963-
   Huron / Barbara A. Gray-Kanatiiosh.
     p. cm. -- (Native Americans)
   Summary: An introduction to the history, social life and customs, and present life of the Huron Indians, a tribe whose homelands centered around the Great Lakes region but now include Kansas and Oklahoma.
   Includes bibliographical references and index.
   ISBN 1-57765-935-X
   1. Wyandot Indians--Juvenile literature. [1. Wyandot Indians. 2. Indians of North America.] I. Title. II. Native Americans (Edina, Minn.)

E99.H9 G53 2003
977.004'9755--dc21

2002027799

About the Author: Barbara A. Gray-Kanatiiosh, JD

Barbara Gray-Kanatiiosh, JD, Ph.D. ABD, is an Akwesasne Mohawk. She resides at the Mohawk Nation and is of the Wolf Clan. She has a Juris Doctorate from Arizona State University, where she was one of the first recipients of ASU's special certificate in Indian Law. Barbara's Ph.D. is in Justice Studies at ASU. She is currently working on her dissertation, which concerns the impacts of environmental injustice on indigenous culture. Barbara works hard to educate children about Native Americans through her writing and Web site, where children may ask questions and receive a written response about the Haudenosaunee culture. The Web site is: www.peace4turtleisland.org

About the Illustrator: David Kanietakeron Fadden

David Kanietakeron Fadden is a member of the Akwesasne Mohawk Wolf Clan. His work has appeared in publications such as *Akwesasne Notes*, *Indian Time*, and the *Northeast Indian Quarterly*. Examples of his work have also appeared in various publications of the Six Nations Indian Museum in Onchiota, NY. His work has also appeared in "How The West Was Lost: Always The Enemy," produced by Gannett Production, which appeared on the Discovery Channel. David's work has been exhibited in Albany, NY; the Lake Placid Center for the Arts; Centre Strathearn in Montreal, Quebec; North Country Community College in Saranac Lake, NY; Paul Smith's College in Paul Smiths, NY; and at the Unison Arts & Learning Center in New Paltz, NY.

Contents

Where They Lived

The Huron's homelands were concentrated in the Great Lakes region. Neighboring tribes included the Iroquois, Tobacco, and Algonquin.

Water bordered Huron territory on three sides. Lake Ontario bordered it to the east, while Lake Erie bordered their territory to the south. West of Huron territory lay Lake Huron.

The Huron's land was **diverse**. It held meadows, mountains, rivers, and lakes. Forests of maple, walnut, birch, and oak grew on these lands. There were also stands of evergreens and **conifers** such as Douglas firs and hemlocks.

Lake Ontario

The Huron spoke a language from the Iroquoian language family. Different Huron bands formed a **confederacy** called the Wendat. The word *Wendat* means "Dwellers of the Peninsula" or "Islanders." Today, several Huron nations take their name from this word.

The name Huron comes from French explorers. The French thought the Wendat's hairstyle looked like the hairs that stand up on a boar's head. In Old French, the word *hure* means "boar's head." Thus, the French called the native people Huron.

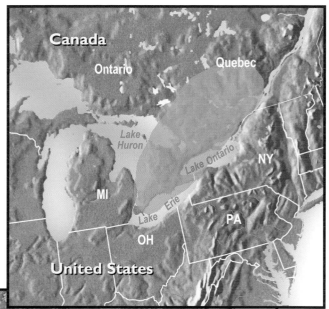

Huron Homelands

Society

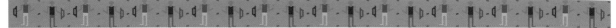

The Huron were originally made up of 12 clans. The clans were the Big Turtle, Striped Turtle, Highland Turtle, Little Turtle, Mud Turtle, Bear, Beaver, Deer, Porcupine, Hawk, Wolf, and Snake.

Each clan had a chief who was responsible for the people. The chief planned hunting and fishing trips. He also consulted with the elders and medicine men before making important decisions.

Huron clans were matrilineal. This means that Huron children belonged to their mother's clan. The Huron clans lived in villages made up of many longhouses. Each longhouse in the village held members of the same clan. Sometimes several families of the same clan lived inside a single longhouse.

The largest longhouse stood at the center of the Huron village. This longhouse was used by the society for political and spiritual gatherings. The village chiefs met there to discuss important matters.

Each Huron village belonged to the Huron **Confederacy**. The Confederacy council of chiefs worked together to protect their people from harm.

The Huron also had religious societies. These societies performed dances and sang songs that they believed kept the people spiritually and politically healthy.

The Confederacy council of chiefs worked together to make important decisions.

Food

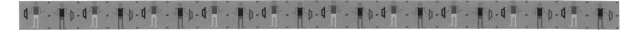

The Huron produced their own food. They gardened, hunted, fished, and gathered wild berries and plants. The Huron gardens contained corn, beans, and squashes. Corn was their main crop. They often ate corn while it was still fresh.

Sometimes, however, the Huron dried the corn. To do this, the women peeled back the corn's husks and braided them together. Then, they hung the connected ears of corn in a dry place.

Once the corn was dry, they placed the kernels inside a hollowed-out log. Then, they ground the kernels into meal with a long, wooden **pestle**. The Huron used the cornmeal for making bread. Sometimes they made soup from water, cornmeal, and dried fish or dried meat.

Corn was also important for Huron warriors. Warriors took roasted corn into battle with them. They could eat the corn for many days, without needing to cook.

Huron men fished using a weir. The fish swam into the weir and became trapped. The men easily speared the trapped fish. They used wooden spears that had three hand-carved **barbs** at one end. The barbs prevented the fish from falling off after being speared.

Men also hunted using bows and arrows, **blowguns**, and snares. They hunted for deer, bears, beavers, and rabbits. They also used handwoven nets to catch ducks and geese.

Dried corn could be ground with a pestle in a hollowed-out log.

Homes

The Huron built homes from natural materials they found in their environment. They lived in bark-covered longhouses. The length of the house depended on how many people were going to live in it. However, a typical longhouse was 100 feet (30 m) long and 30 feet (9 m) wide.

To make a longhouse, the Huron buried the ends of sapling poles in the ground. They bent the poles to create a frame shaped like an upside-down U. Next, they used rope made from natural fibers to attach cross poles to the frame. The cross poles strengthened the framework. The Huron used more cross poles to hold slabs of cedar bark onto the frame.

At each end of the longhouse was a door covered with a woven mat. With red paint, the Huron painted **pictographs** above the door. The pictographs could be symbols of clans, or just decorative artwork. The Huron made the red paint from red **ocher**. Corn crops surrounded the longhouses. The Huron built **palisades** around their longhouse villages for protection.

Inside the longhouse, the Huron used fire pits for cooking and warmth. Openings in the roof let light inside and helped the smoke escape. Two large poles in the middle of the longhouse held racks for storing food and cooking tools. The people slept on platforms. The platforms were usually four to five feet (1 to 2 m) high. The longhouse's floor was lined with bark.

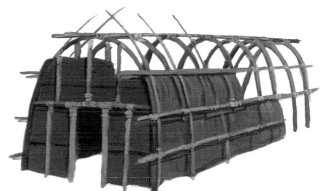

The building of a Huron longhouse

Clothing

The Huron made clothing from animals and plants they found in their environment. They took **sinew** from a deer and used it for thread. The Huron made needles from the shinbone of a deer.

The Huron made a great majority of their clothing from deerskin. They decorated their clothing with moose-hair embroidery and porcupine quillwork. They also painted symbols and designs on their clothing with red paint.

Men wore deerskin **breechcloths** or **kilts** and moccasins. They wore sashes over the left shoulder and tied them on the right at the waist. These sashes were finger woven from plant fibers. Sometimes Huron men wore a turban or feathered hat on their heads.

In colder weather, men wore deerskin shirts with long fringes on the bottom. They also wore waist- or thigh-high leggings. The leggings protected their legs from the cold and from thorns while hunting.

The Huron also wore fur shirts and black fox fur robes in cold weather. They wore these robes with the fur touching the skin. This kept the Huron warm because fur traps body heat.

Women wore deerskin dresses and moccasins. They also wore deerskin mantles, skirts, and knee-high leggings. The mantles tied around the neck and hung down to the skirt top.

Huron clothing

Crafts

The Huron were skilled **artisans**. They used materials from the animals that they had hunted. For example, moose provided the Huron with hides for robes and hair for decorating clothing.

The Huron sorted and dyed the moose hair. They used natural dyes from items such as bloodroot, walnut shells, and berries. With a fine needle, the women embroidered the dyed moose hair into beautiful geometric and floral designs. They decorated the pouches worn by men, as well as shirts and moccasins.

Moose hair was not the only material used in Huron decoration. Huron women also gathered porcupine guard hairs. They tied these hairs together to form tassels. They often dyed the tassels red and added them to clothing for decoration.

After the Huron began trading with Europeans, they used glass beads and cloth in their crafts. In addition, they began making moose-hair embroidered jewelry for trade. Today, some Huron continue to do porcupine and moose-hair work.

This Huron woman uses natural materials for her craft.

Family

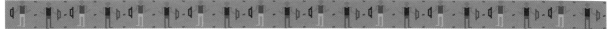

Family was important to the Huron. Members of an extended family lived together inside a longhouse. Each member contributed to the survival of the family by helping with daily chores. The Huron men and women each had different responsibilities.

Men hunted and fished. They journeyed to neighboring nations to trade extra food, clothing, and hides. Men also planted tobacco, which was burned to give thanks.

Huron men made hunting and fishing tools, such as spears and bows and arrows. Men used a stone **adze** to harvest trees and bark for building longhouses. After the Huron began trading with Europeans, Huron men used metal tools. Metal tools were more durable, and they cut faster than stone tools.

Women tended large gardens. They prepared the soil with small wooden shovels and hoes. The hoes were made from the shoulder blade of a deer attached to a wooden handle. Women planted corn, beans, and squashes. They also planted sunflowers.

They made the sunflower seeds into oil, which was used as a skin and hair lotion.

Women also gathered wild vegetables, nuts, and berries. They gathered medicinal plants, too. The Huron either took the medicine right away, or dried it to use later.

The elders were the wisdom keepers. They often told stories that taught **cultural** lessons. It was a great time for the family to come together. Story time was both fun and educational.

A Huron elder tells his story to eager listeners.

Children

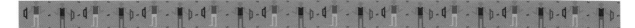

    Children learned by helping the adults with daily tasks. Boys watched the men and helped make tools for hunting and fishing. Boys were often given toy bows and arrows and fishing spears. Playing with the toys helped them develop the skills they needed for hunting and fishing.

    Girls learned how to tend gardens by helping the women. They learned how deep to plant the seeds. They also learned where to find and how to pick plants that they could eat. Girls played with dolls and small **cradleboards**. These toys helped them learn how to care for a family.

    In June, the children helped their parents gather long, wide rolls of birch bark. At this time of the year, they could cut some layers of the bark without harming the tree. The Huron then used the bark to make birch bark canoes, baskets, containers, cups, and spoons.

Children also played games. They had running games that kept their legs and hearts strong. Another game they played was like today's football. The children also played lacrosse. This game was played with a ball and a long, curved racket with a net at one end.

A Huron boy hunts with a bow and arrow.

Myths

During the winter, Huron families gathered around the fire for warmth. At this time, the Huron told many stories. One of these stories is about how the earth was created.

A long time ago, the entire planet was covered by water. In the Water World lived animal beings that looked like many of today's creatures. Above, in the Sky World, lived beings that looked very much like today's humans.

There was a loud clap of thunder. Two passing loons heard the roar and looked up. They were surprised by what they saw falling from the sky. It was a sky woman. She was falling from a hole in the Sky World.

The loons realized that they must help this beautiful woman before she fell to her death. The loons interlaced their wings and formed a place to hold the sky woman. The sky woman landed safely on their wings. She was very thankful.

The water animals, seeing what had happened, called a meeting to discuss what to do. They called the Big Turtle. Big Turtle offered his back so the sky woman could have a place to stand.

Soon animals began to dive for mud from the bottom of the water.

The sky woman took the mud from one of the animals and placed it on the turtle's back. Suddenly, the mud began to grow. The Huron believe that is how Turtle Island, their name for North and South America, was created.

A sky woman tumbles from the Sky World.

War

The Huron created the Huron **Confederacy** to help protect their lands and people. During the French and Indian War, the Huron Confederacy helped the French. During the American Revolution, the Huron helped the British.

Huron fought with wooden war clubs, bows and arrows, and knives. The Huron were protected by wearing wooden armor. They made it by tying together small pieces of wood. They also used cedar bark shields to protect themselves during war. This armor worked well until European traders introduced metal and guns.

Before going to war, warriors asked a medicine man to do a ceremony for them. He performed the ceremony to protect the warriors from being harmed during the fight. If a group of warriors became trapped in a battle, the older men would stay and fight as the younger men escaped.

The wooden armor of
the Huron at war

Contact with Europeans

The Huron had strong trade relations with other tribes before European contact. Then in 1608, French explorer Samuel de Champlain traveled from France to found the city of Quebec. He eventually entered Huron territory.

Champlain saw the strength of the Huron and wanted to create an **alliance** with them. He thought converting the Huron to Christianity would be the best way to develop this alliance. He convinced the Huron to allow Jesuits to build missions within Huron territory. He also built trading posts and settlements within **Huronia**.

Contact with Europeans changed the Huron way of life in other ways, too. European settlers brought new illnesses to North America. The Huron had no **immunity** to some of these sicknesses. Around 1634, deadly smallpox **epidemics** killed many Huron.

The fur trade also created problems. European traders wanted beaver **pelts** to ship back to France and England. As beaver numbers dwindled, competition and tension grew between the Iroquois and the Huron.

Matters worsened when European traders supplied the tribes with guns and alcohol. During this time, the Huron lost about 75 percent of their population to war and disease.

Samuel de Champlain meets a Huron man.

Tarhe

Tarhe (tar-HAY) was a famous Huron chief. He was born in 1714 and was a member of the Porcupine clan. The word *Tarhe* means "the tree" or "at the tree." People also called him "the crane" because he was tall and slender.

In his youth, Tarhe was a respected warrior. Later in his life, he was selected to become a chief. Tarhe fought hard to protect his people, **culture**, and lands. He also worked toward creating peace between the Europeans and his people.

When Tarhe died in 1816, he had one of the biggest funerals ever seen by the Huron and neighboring nations. Many famous leaders such as the Seneca Nation's Chief Red Jacket attended the funeral. The Huron and other nations respected him for working toward peace.

Chief Tarhe

27

The Huron Today

Disease and war hurt the Huron. They struggled to keep their beliefs alive as Jesuit missionaries worked to convert them to Christianity. Many people today even believe that the Huron language is dead.

A statue commemorates the Huron who worked with Champlain.

However, the Huron are working hard to bring back their language and to strengthen their **culture**. Recently, they reaffirmed the Huron **Confederacy**. Today, there are Huron reservations in Canada and the United States.

In Canada, there is a reserve located in Quebec and a settlement near Sandwich, Ontario. The Wendake Reserve is located north of Quebec City, in the province of Quebec. About 2,791 Huron live at Wendake.

In the United States, there are three Huron nations. They are the Wyandot Nation of Kansas, the Wyandotte Nation of Oklahoma, and the Wyandot of Anderdon Nation in Michigan.

The Wyandotte Nation of Oklahoma is the only **federally recognized** Huron reservation in the United States. The Wyandot of Kansas and the Anderdon Nation of Michigan are continuing to seek federal recognition. Today, the Huron continue working to preserve their **culture**.

Head carvings at the Huron Indian Village, a museum in Ontario

Today, the traditional Huron way of life is maintained by Huron village museums such as this one in Midland, Ontario.

Glossary

adze - a tool that looks similar to an ax. It is used for shaping and trimming wood.

alliance - people, groups, or nations joined for a common cause.

artisan - a person skilled in a craft or trade.

barb - a sharp point reaching backward.

blowgun - a tube through which a person blows darts or arrows.

breechcloth - a piece of hide or cloth, usually worn by men, that wraps between the legs and ties with a belt around the waist.

confederacy - a group of people joined together for a common purpose.

conifer - a tree or shrub that bears needles or cones and keeps its needles in the winter.

cradleboard - a flat board used to hold a baby. It could be carried on the mother's back or hung from a tree so that the baby could see what was going on.

culture - the customs, arts, and tools of a nation or people at a certain time.

diverse - composed of several distinct pieces or qualities.

epidemic - the rapid spread of a disease among many people.

federal recognition - the U.S. government's recognition of a tribe as being an independent nation. The tribe is then eligible for special funding and for protection of its reservation lands.

Huronia - the land of the Huron.

immunity - protection against disease.

kilt - a knee-length, skirt-like garment worn by men.

ocher - a red or yellow iron ore used for color.

palisade - a fence of strong stakes placed closely together and set firmly into the ground.

pelt - an animal skin with the fur still on it.

pestle - a club-shaped tool used to pound or crush a substance.

pictograph - a picture that represents a word or idea.

sinew - a band of tough fibers that joins a muscle to a bone.

Web Sites

To learn more about the Huron, visit ABDO Publishing Company on the World Wide Web at **www.abdopub.com**. Web sites about the Huron are featured on our Book Links page. These links are routinely monitored and updated to provide the most current information available.

Index